BUDDHISM IS THE CLEAR MIRROR
THAT REFLECTS OUR LIVES

Daisaku Ikeda

World Tribune
Press

Published by
World Tribune Press
606 Wilshire Blvd.
Santa Monica, CA 90401

© 2014 by the Soka Gakkai

Design by Gopa & Ted2, Inc.
Cover image © Photodisc

ISBN 978-1-935523-71-0

10 9 8 7

SGI President Ikeda
at the first SGI-USA women's division meeting,
Soka University of America,
Calabasas, California, February 27, 1990.

BUDDHISM IS THE CLEAR MIRROR
THAT REFLECTS OUR LIVES

At the first SGI-USA women's division meeting,
Soka University of America,
Calabasas, California, February 27, 1990

I SINCERELY THANK all of you for gathering here from distant places throughout the United States. My sole desire for women's division members is that they become the happiest people in the world.

What is the purpose of life? It is happiness. There are two kinds of happiness, however: relative and absolute. Relative happiness comes in a wide variety of forms. The purpose of Buddhism is to attain Buddhahood, which in modern terms could be understood as realizing absolute happiness — a state of happiness that can never be destroyed or defeated.

Nichiren Daishonin states in his writings, "There is no true happiness for human beings other than chanting Nam-myoho-renge-kyo" (WND-1, 681). So long as you maintain strong faith, resolutely chanting daimoku to the Gohonzon no matter what happens, then without fail you will be able to lead a life of complete fulfillment.

This accords with the principle that "earthly desires are enlightenment."

True happiness lies only in establishing such a supreme state of life. In so doing, you can change all sufferings into causes for joy and contentment, and live with composure and jubilation.

Our organization exists so that each member can attain absolute happiness. Let me reiterate that the objective of this organization is your happiness.

Society and daily life are the "great earth" for our faith and practice of the correct teaching. The steady development of world peace can be ensured only when, based on faith, we carefully attend to the affairs of society, our daily lives, and our families. Faith manifests itself in daily life — this is our eternal guideline.

I would like to take this opportunity to introduce to you some treasures in the collection of Soka University. This is my way of commemorating today's women's division meeting and showing my appreciation to you for your attendance. Afterward, please take a moment to look them over. Included are letters by George Washington and other American presidents, on display with their portraits; a collection of letters that Napoleon Bonaparte wrote just before his death and a letter in which he appealed for religious freedom in Italy; an autographed first edition of Victor Hugo's anthology of poems *Les Châtiments* (1853), along with some of Hugo's letters;

a letter from British historian Arnold J. Toynbee to former U.S. Secretary of State John Foster Dulles appealing for peace in Pakistan; a letter in which the German composer Richard Wagner discusses the performance of his opera *Tannhauser* (1845); a state document signed by John Hancock, a political leader during the American Revolution; and a letter written by Bartolomeo Vanzetti, dated immediately before his execution on trumped-up charges (1927), which contains a plea for a retrial. If he were executed, he wrote, the court would be guilty of murder. We can hear the cry of his soul for liberation.

These articles represent a precious, historic legacy. As part of the SGI's efforts to promote peace, culture, and education, we are preserving and introducing these and other artifacts to the public. For the same purpose, we are establishing the Maison Littéraire de Victor Hugo (Victor Hugo House of Literature) in France. I am convinced that these activities will be of great significance for the future of humanity.

The Mirror That Perfectly Reflects Our Lives

I hope that all of you will be cultured and graceful. Intelligent and kind people are beautiful. They inspire trust and a sense of reassurance in those around them. As you continue to deepen your faith in Buddhism, you can broaden your sphere of knowledge.

Without wisdom and sagacity, leaders cannot fulfill their mission — that is, convince others of the power of Nichiren Daishonin's Buddhism and help them attain true happiness. In this sense, I would like to speak about the correct attitude in faith through the analogy of mirrors.

A Japanese proverb has it that the mirror is a woman's soul. It is said that just as warriors will never part with their swords, women will never part with their mirrors. There would seem to be some truth to this saying, in that mirrors are prized by women the world over.

In Buddhism, the mirror is used to explain various doctrines. In one place, Nichiren Daishonin states, "There are various sayings associated with mirrors" (OTT, 51). In another of his writings, he states: "A bronze mirror will reflect the form of a person but it will not reflect that person's mind. The Lotus Sutra, however, reveals not only the person's form but that person's mind as well. And it reveals not only the mind; it reflects, without the least concealment, that person's past actions and future as well" (WND-2, 619).

Mirrors reflect our outward form. The mirror of Buddhism, however, reveals the intangible aspect of our lives. Mirrors, which function by virtue of the laws of light and reflection, are a product of human wisdom. On the other hand, the Gohonzon, based on the law of the universe and life itself, is the culmination of the

Buddha's wisdom and makes it possible for us to attain Buddhahood by providing us with a means of perceiving the true aspect of our life. Just as a mirror is indispensable for putting your face and hair in order, you need a mirror that reveals the depths of your life if you are to lead a happier and more beautiful existence.

Incidentally, as indicated in the Daishonin's reference to a bronze mirror in the above passage, mirrors in ancient times were made of polished metal alloys such as bronze, nickel, and steel. The oldest metallic mirrors to be unearthed were found in China and Egypt. Older still are mirrors made of polished stone surfaces and those that used water. Suffice it to say that the history of mirrors is as old as that of the human race. It is perhaps an inborn human instinct to want to look at one's face.

These ancient mirrors, unlike today's mirrors that are made of glass, could only produce somewhat blurred reflections of images. Consequently, the first glance in a glass mirror caused a great sensation. The first time the Japanese encountered a glass mirror was in 1551. Francis Xavier is credited with having brought one with him when he came to do missionary work in Japan.

It was not until the eighteenth century, however, that the average Japanese became acquainted with this kind of mirror. Perhaps because it performed its function all too well, causing people to do nothing but gaze in the mirror all day long, the glass mirror came to be known as the "vanity mirror" among the people of the day. Many prints from this era depict Japanese beauties gazing into mirrors. Still, it was not until the latter half of the nineteenth century that glass mirrors came into wide use among the general populace.

Polish the Mirror of Your Life

Bronze mirrors not only reflected poorly but also tarnished very quickly. Therefore, unless they were polished regularly, they became unusable. This kind of mirror was popular in the time when the Daishonin lived.

In "On Attaining Buddhahood in This Lifetime," Nichiren Daishonin writes: "This is similar to a tarnished mirror that will shine like a jewel when polished. A mind now clouded by the illusions of the innate darkness of life is like a tarnished mirror, but when polished, it is sure to become like a clear mirror, reflecting the essential nature of phenomena and the true aspect of reality" (WND-1, 4). In this well-known passage, the Daishonin draws parallels between the tradition of mirror-polishing and the process of attaining Buddhahood.

Originally, every person's life is a brilliantly shining mirror. Differences arise depending on whether one polishes this mirror. A polished mirror is the Buddha's life, whereas a tarnished mirror is that of a common mortal. Chanting Nam-myoho-renge-kyo is what polishes our life. Not only do we undertake this practice ourselves, we also endeavor to teach others about the Mystic Law so that the mirror of their lives shines brightly too. Thus it can be said that we are masters of the art of polishing the mirror of life.

Even though people may make up their faces, they tend to neglect to polish their lives. While they quickly wash off a stain from their face, they remain unconcerned about stains in their lives.

The Tragedy of Dorian Gray

Oscar Wilde (1854–1900) wrote a novel titled *The Picture of Dorian Gray*, whose protagonist, a youth named Dorian Gray, is so handsome that he is called a "young Adonis." An artist who wished to preserve his beauty for eternity painted Dorian's portrait. It was a brilliant work, an embodiment of Dorian's youthfulness and beauty. Then something incredible occurred as Dorian was gradually tempted by a friend into a life of hedonism and immorality: His beauty did not fade. Although he advanced in years, he remained as youthful and radiant as ever. Strangely, however, the portrait began to turn ugly and lusterless, reflecting the condition of Dorian's life.

Making sport of a young woman's affections, Dorian drives her to commit suicide. At that time, the face of the portrait takes on a wicked, savage, and frightening expression. Dorian is filled with horror. This portrait of his soul would remain for aeons in this ugly form. Even if he died, the portrait would continue to eloquently tell the truth.

Dorian decides to obliterate the portrait, believing that if only he could do away with it, he could part with his past and be free. So he plunges a knife into the painting. At that moment, hearing screams, his neighbors rush over to find a portrait of the handsome, young Dorian and, collapsed before it, an aged, repulsive-looking man, Dorian, with a knife sticking in his chest.

The portrait had expressed the semblance of his existence, the face of his soul, into which the effects of his actions were etched without the slightest omission.

Though cosmetics can be applied to the face, one cannot gloss over the face of his soul. The law of cause and effect functioning in the depths of life is strict and impartial.

Buddhism teaches that unseen virtue brings about visible reward. In the world of Buddhism, one never fails to receive an effect for one's actions — whether for good or bad; therefore, it is meaningless to be two-faced or to try to put on airs.

The face of the soul that is etched by the good and evil causes one makes is to an extent reflected in one's appearance. There is also a saying "The face is the mirror of the mind." It is at the moment of death, however, that one's past causes show most plainly in one's appearance. Just as Dorian in the end revealed his own inner ugliness, so the "face of one's life" is fully expressed at the time of one's death. At that time, there is no way to conceal the truth of your soul. We carry out our Buddhist practice now so that we will not have to experience any regret or torment on our deathbed.

Perceive the Buddha Nature Inherent in Your Life

Just as you look into a mirror when you make up your face, to beautify the face of the soul, you need a mirror that reflects the depths of your life. This mirror is none other than the Gohonzon of "observing one's mind," or more precisely, observing one's life. Nichiren Daishonin explains what it means to observe one's life in "The Object of Devotion for Observing the Mind": "Only when we look into a clear mirror do we see, for the first time, that we are endowed with all six sense organs" (WND-1, 356).

Similarly, observing one's life means to perceive that one's life contains the Ten Worlds and, in particular, the world of Buddhahood. It was to enable people to do this that Nichiren Daishonin bestowed the Gohonzon of "observing one's mind" upon all humankind. In his exegesis on "The Object of Devotion for Observing the Mind," Nichikan, the twenty-sixth chief priest of Taiseki-ji, states, "The true object of devotion can be compared to a wonderful mirror."

Nichiren Daishonin states in *The Record of the Orally Transmitted Teachings,* "The five characters of Myoho-renge-kyo similarly reflect the ten thousand phenomena, not overlooking a single one of them" (OTT, 51). The Gohonzon is the clearest of all mirrors that reflects the entire universe exactly as it is. When you chant to the Gohonzon, you can perceive the true aspect of your life and tap the inexhaustible life force of Buddhahood.

Incidentally, the glass mirrors that we have today are said to have been invented in Venice, Italy. Sources differ as to exactly when, but their appearance is traced as far back as 1279. That was also the year when Nichiren Daishonin inscribed the Dai-Gohonzon, the eternal great "mirror" reflecting the true aspect of all phenomena, for the benefit of all humanity.

At the time of the glass mirror's invention, the production technique was said to have been kept a closely guarded secret in Italy. To prevent knowledge of the technology from spreading, mirror glass craftsmen were confined to an island. Before long, however, France and other countries learned how to produce mirrors, and today mirrors made of glass have completely replaced earlier types.

These events might be construed as the "kosen-rufu of the glass mirror." Similarly, for a long time, the mirror of the Gohonzon, the source of profound beauty and happiness, was known to very few people. We are now promoting the movement to spread it widely.

The Gohonzon is a clear mirror. It perfectly reveals our state of faith and projects this out into the universe. This demonstrates the principle of "three thousand realms in a single moment of life."

One's Mind of Faith Is Most Important

In a letter to his disciple Abutsu-bo on Sado Island, Nichiren Daishonin wrote: "You may think you offered gifts to the treasure tower of the Thus Come One Many Treasures, but that is not so. You offered them to yourself" (WND-1, 299). Chanting to the Gohonzon graces and glorifies the treasure tower of your own life.

When people chant to the Gohonzon, all Buddhas and bodhisattvas in the entire universe immediately respond to their prayers by lending their protection. If they slander the Gohonzon, the response will be exactly the opposite.

For this reason, one's mind of faith is extremely

important. The mind of faith has a subtle and far-reaching influence.

There may be times, for instance, when you feel reluctant to do gongyo or take part in activities. That state of mind is precisely reflected on the entire universe, as if on the surface of a clear mirror. The heavenly deities will then also feel reluctant to play their part, and they will naturally fail to exert their full power of protection.

On the other hand, when you joyfully do gongyo and carry out activities with the determination to accumulate more good fortune in your life, the heavenly deities will be delighted and will valiantly perform their duty. If you must take some action anyway, it is to your advantage that you do so spontaneously and with a feeling of joy. If you practice reluctantly with a sense that it's a waste of time, disbelief and complaints will erode your good fortune. If you continue to practice in this way, you will not experience remarkable benefits, and this will only serve to further convince you that your practice is in vain. This is a vicious circle.

If you practice faith while doubting its effects, you will get results that are, at best, unsatisfactory. This is the reflection of your own weak faith on the mirror of the cosmos.

On the other hand, when you stand up with strong confidence, you will accrue limitless blessings. While controlling your mind, which is at once both extremely subtle and solemnly profound, you should strive to elevate your faith with freshness and vigor. When you do so, both your life and your surroundings will open wide before you, and every action you take will become a source of benefit. Understanding the subtle workings of one's mind is the key to faith and to attaining Buddhahood in this lifetime.

There is a Russian proverb that says, "It is no use to blame the looking glass if your face is awry." Likewise, your happiness or unhappiness is entirely the reflection of the balance of good and bad causes accumulated in your life. You cannot blame others for your misfortunes. In the world of faith, it is necessary to realize this all the more clearly.

People Who Do Not Know About Mirrors

A classic Japanese comedy tells the following story: Once there was a country village where no one had a mirror. In those days, mirrors were priceless. A man, returning from his trip to the capital, handed his wife a mirror as a souvenir. That was the first time for her to see a mirror. Looking into it, she exclaimed: "Who on earth is this woman? You must've brought a girl back with you from the capital." And so began a big fight.

Though this story is fictitious, many people become angry or grieve over phenomena that are actually nothing but the reflection of their own lives — their state of mind and the causes that they have created. Like the wife in the story who exclaims, "Who on earth is this woman?" they do not realize the folly of their ways.

Because they are ignorant of Buddhism's mirror of life, such people cannot see themselves as they truly are. This being the case, they cannot guide others along the correct path of life nor can they discern the true nature of occurrences in society.

Mutual Respect

Human relations also function as a kind of mirror. Nichiren Daishonin states in *The Record of the Orally Transmitted Teachings*: "When the bodhisattva Never Disparaging makes his bow of obeisance to the four kinds of believers, the Buddha nature inherent in the four kinds of believers of overbearing arrogance is bowing in obeisance to the bodhisattva Never Disparaging. It is like the situation when one faces a mirror and makes a bow of obeisance: the image in the mirror likewise makes a bow of obeisance to oneself" (OTT, 165).

Here, the Daishonin reveals the fundamental spirit that we should have in propagating the Mystic Law. Propagation is an act to be conducted with the utmost

18

respect for other people and out of sincere reverence for the Buddha nature inherent in their lives. Therefore, we should strictly observe courtesy and good common sense.

With the thought that we are addressing a person's Buddha nature, we should politely and calmly carry out a dialogue — sometimes, depending on the situation, mercifully correcting that person with fatherly strictness. In the course of such human interaction, the Buddha nature in that person, reflecting our own sincerity, will bow to us in return.

When we cherish that person with the same profound reverence as we would the Buddha, the Buddha nature in his or her life functions to protect us. On the other hand, if we belittle or regard that person with contempt, we will be disparaged in return, as though our actions are being reflected in a mirror.

In the inner realm of life, cause and effect occur simultaneously. With the passage of time, this causal relationship becomes manifest in the phenomenal world of daily life.

In general, the people around us reflect our state of life. Our personal preferences, for example, are mirrored in their attitudes. This is especially clear from the viewpoint of Buddhism, which elucidates the workings of cause and effect as if in a spotless mirror.

To the extent that you praise, respect, protect, and

care for SGI-USA members, who are all children of the Buddha, you will in turn be protected by the Buddhas and bodhisattvas of the ten directions and by all heavenly deities. If, on the other hand, you are arrogant or condescending toward members, you will be scolded by the Buddhas and others in like measure. Leaders, in particular, should be clear on this point and take it deeply to heart.

We are a gathering of the Buddha's children. Therefore, if we respect one another, our good fortune will multiply infinitely, like an image reflected back and forth among mirrors. A person who practices alone cannot experience this tremendous multiplication of benefit.

In short, the environment that you find yourself in, whether favorable or not, is the product of your own life. Most people, however, fail to understand this and tend to blame others for their troubles. Nichiren Daishonin states: "These people, failing to recognize their own rudeness, seem to think that I am rude. They are like a jealous woman with furious eyes who, unaware that when she glares at a courtesan her own expression is disagreeable, instead complains that the courtesan's gaze is frightening" (WND-1, 828). The Daishonin explains human psychology in such a clear and easy-to-understand manner.

There are people who, out of malice, have criticized and sought to oppress us, the Daishonin's disciples. But, reflected in the mirror of the world of the Mystic Law, such people see only their own faults, ambitions, and greed and therefore slander their own reflections. To a person who is possessed by the lust for power, even the most selfless, benevolent actions of others will appear as cunning moves undertaken to gain power. Similarly, to a person who has a strong desire for fame, actions based on conviction and consideration will be seen as publicity stunts. Those who have become slaves of money simply cannot believe that there are people in the world who are strangers to the desire for wealth.

In contrast, an unusually kind and good-natured person will tend to believe that all others are the same. To a greater or lesser extent, all people tend to see their own reflection in others.

In the SGI-USA, there are a great number of people who are full of good will and intentions. In a sense, some might be even too good-natured and trusting — to the extent that I fear deceitful people could mislead them.

Say What Must Be Said

In *Père Goriot,* the French author Balzac (1799–1850) writes, "Whatever evil you hear of society, believe it. . . ." So full of evil was the world that he perceived. He adds: "And then you will find out what the world is, a gathering of dupes and rogues. Be of neither party."

We must gain decisive victory over the harsh realities of society and lead a correct and vibrant life. This is the purpose of our faith. We have to become wise and strong.

Also, in the organization for kosen-rufu, we have to clearly say what must be said. The purpose of Buddhism is not to produce dupes who blindly follow their leaders. Rather, it is to produce people of wisdom who can judge right or wrong on their own in the clear mirror of Buddhism.

I hope that you, women's division members, learn the correct way to practice Buddhism so that, in the event that a leader or a man does something that goes against reason, you will be able to clearly point out the error and identify the correct path to follow. Nichiren Daishonin compares men to an arrow and women to the bow. An arrow flies in the direction that the bow points it.

I would like to tell you that when the members of the women's division freely devote themselves to activities and provide a confident and strong lead for the men, that will mark the dawn of the "new SGI-USA."

To commemorate today's training session, I would like to dedicate the following poem to the SGI-USA women's division:

Let the flowers of the Law
Bloom with beauty and purity
Throughout this land of America.

I close my speech by offering my sincere prayers for the happiness of you and your families, and for the further development of the SGI-USA.